W9-AWX-346

Stress
Just Chill Out!

Joe anne Adler

Enslow Publishers, Inc.

44 Fadem Road   PO Box 38
Box 699   Aldershot
Springfield, NJ 07081   Hants GU12 6BP
USA   UK

Library of Congress Cataloging-in-Publication Data

Adler, Joe anne.
    Stress: just chill out! / Joe anne Adler
      p. cm.
    Includes bibliographical references and index.
    Summary: Discusses the causes and symptoms of teenage stress and ways of
measuring and dealing with it.
    ISBN 0-89490-918-5
    1. Stress in adolescence—Juvenile literature. 2. Stress management for teenagers—
Juvenile literature. [1. Stress (Psychology)] I. Title
BF724.3.S86A35   1997
155.9'042—dc20   96-32678
                                    CIP
                                      AC

Printed in the United States of America

10 9 8 7 6 5 4 3 2 1

Cover Illustration: © Eric Berndt/UNICORN STOCK PHOTOS

I have read *Stress: Just Chill Out!* and I believe it is a sound resource book on this important subject. Readers will find here reliable information that could help them cope with similar situations in their own lives.

—*Stephen P. Herman, M.D.*
Associate Clinical Professor of Psychiatry
Yale Child Study Center

Contents

Author's Note

Being a teenager is not easy. Through the course of your development you will experience times in which you feel lost, alone, overwhelmed, fed up, angry, and hurt. But please do not give up; as I mention in this book, "No one is fifteen forever." The vignettes that I use in this book are based upon actual events that happened to students with whom I worked when I was a counselor at several different schools. I have, of course, changed the names and altered the descriptions so they can remain anonymous. As far as I know all of these young people have made it into adulthood. For some, the journey was very difficult for several years; for others, adolescence was more tolerable.

Stress: Just Chill Out! is designed to give you information, and perhaps as you read it you will wonder if all those facts are really necessary. The purpose of all the research material quoted in this book is to help you understand two very important aspects of stress. The first is that stress and all the physical, emotional, mental, and behavioral changes it causes are natural consequences of life. In other words, if you are alive, you will experience stress. The second important aspect is that YOU have within your power the ability, skill, and strength to manage stress!

I would like to thank Matt Clukies who helped shape the first draft of the book; my husband, Jay, for all his support; and my three grown children Jessica, Jennifer, and Jason who taught me many years ago about adolescent stress.

1

Signs and Symptoms of Teenage Stress

Marsha, Jeff, and Jenny, whose stories follow, are typical American teenagers who are under stress. Life in the 1990s for them and millions of other teenagers in the United States is not without its difficulties. Teenagers today are faced with pressure all around them. In addition to coping with the tremendous changes that are taking place within their own bodies, teenagers are bombarded with pressures from friendships, achievements, academics, appropriate dress, parental expectations, house rules, and life in general. These pressures can cause teen stress.

Entering her house, Marsha could feel the knot in her throat. She was tired from a full day at school that included a history test, a pop quiz in geometry, and a detention slip for being late for English class and for losing her assignment notebook. As she stepped inside her house she heard her mother's voice yelling and the sound of the phone being slammed down. Marsha felt a sharp pain in her stomach as she caught her mother's eye. "Where have you been, school has been over for more than an hour?" Marsha could feel her heart pounding, but she tried to downplay her lateness and answered, "I had to stay after for a while." Her mother jumped in. "Did you get in trouble again? What was it this time?" Marsha walked briskly past her mother, ran up the stairs, and slammed her bedroom door closed before bursting into tears.

Jeff was in the locker room changing into his practice suit. His face was flushed, and he felt sweaty. It was Thursday and the last day of basketball practice before the game Friday night. Today had been really tough for Jeff. It was his first day back at school since the death of his younger brother last week. He felt overwhelmed and uncomfortable around his friends. He bit his inner lip and tried to hide among the lockers in the gym so his teammates wouldn't see him. He felt the tears well up in his eyes as he clenched his fists tighter. He just couldn't take another person saying he was sorry. Being sorry couldn't bring Kevin back.

Jenny dashed out of school and frantically looked for her bus . . . but it had already left. She dropped her backpack, kicked it hard with her foot, and yelled, "I did it again. I hate this." She was angry with herself and could feel the beginning of a headache. Now she would have to walk home and would be late for her afterschool baby-sitting job. She wasn't looking forward to listening to Mrs. Grady chastise her for being late again.

We've All Heard the Word "Stress"— But What Is It?

Stress has been defined as the physical and chemical response of the body to any demand made upon it.[1] That demand includes good things, such as winning a class election, and bad things, such as being picked on by the class bully. The body's mechanical response is the same; the only difference is the intensity of the response and the length of the response. When good things happen to us, like sinking the hoop in an important basketball game or being chosen for the pep squad, the body's reaction is short, complete, and most often not as intense as the body's reaction when facing fearful or bad stress. Whether the stressor (the collective name for any demand) is good or bad, the body's reaction is stress.

Stress can be imposed by external demands, like parental expectations, deadlines, and peer pressure. It can also be generated from within by a teenager's own expectations and goals. Regardless of whether the demands are internal or external, when adolescents perceive that the demands exceed the resources they think they have, their nervous systems activate a special response that disrupts normal body functions and produces physical and chemical changes within their bodies. These changes are called the General Adaptation Syndrome and are the body's way of preparing itself to deal with the new demand.

Through laboratory experiments scientists have been able for many years to document the physical changes that stress produces within the human body. But scientific data on stress's effect on people's social behavior have been more difficult to obtain. It has only been in the last thirty years that researchers have looked upon stress as a multiple manifestation of symptoms and reactions.[2]

Hans Selye's Discovery

One of the first researchers to define stress in relationship to changes within the human body was Hans Selye. In the late 1940s and early 1950s Selye, through experimentation on laboratory rats, observed that animals reacted to stressors—demands or changes within their environment—in a predictable way. He charted the biological changes in the rats' bodies and concluded that when rats were exposed to a variety of stressors their bodies underwent three specific reactions that he called the stage of alarm, the stage of resistance, and the stage of exhaustion. Selye referred to the three stages as the General Adaptation Syndrome and concluded that when humans are exposed to stressors their bodies react in similar ways.[3]

How the General Adaptive Syndrome Works in Teens

Stage of Alarm. During the alarm stage a teen senses that something or someone is threatening or making a demand on his or her mental, emotional, or physical being. This stressor can be a mother who challenges why her adolescent is late from school, a peer criticizing a teen's new haircut, or a mugger with a gun. The more threatening the demand is, the more intensely the body will respond during the alarm stage.

In anticipation of dealing with these stressors, the brain automatically sends a signal to the pituitary and then on to the adrenal gland to increase production of stress steroids, such as ACTH and corticosteroids, which channel all the body's energies to deal with the stressor. This causes physical changes in the normal functions of the heart, stomach, kidneys, lungs, liver, bones, muscles, and brain. The body stops storing energy and begins to call upon its reserves of glucose (sugar), fatty acids, and carbohydrates. The heart rate increases and the spleen contracts and releases glucose, which is stored in the liver. The blood is redirected from the skin to the muscles and brain. Respiration deepens and oxygen intake by the lungs is increased as bronchial tubes expand. Blood is pumped around the body more rapidly and the blood's oxygen-carrying capacity is increased. The skin begins to perspire and salivation decreases, causing dry mouth.[4] Digestion, metabolism, respiration, and blood pressure are affected because of the increase in the production of adrenalin, cortisone, corticosteroids, ACTH, and other hormones. When the body is engaged in the General Adaptation Syndrome, these chemicals are used to help the body mobilize all of its defenses so that the teenager is now ready to take action against the perceived stressor.[5]

Stage of Resistance. Once the actual recognition of the stressor occurs, and the teen is able to evaluate the situation, the body enters the resistance stage. It makes adjustments and its heightened arousal state is somewhat reduced. The body tries to seek a level of alertness equal to the perceived stressor in an attempt to adapt to the stressor. The more threatening or demanding the stressor, the longer the body will remain in the resistance stage. The heart rate decreases but still remains above the normal level. Breathing becomes less pronounced and the bronchial tubes less distended. The blood supply to the brain returns to a more normal level and circulation to the skin improves. Since the body has not returned to its normal state, it continues to produce stress hormones and continues to use up its stored energy. If the perceived stressor is prolonged, or the teenager is subjected to a continual series of stressors or demands, the body's supply of stored energy will diminish. The chemical imbalance caused by the heightened arousal state begins to cause physical, emotional, and mental ailments—such as headaches, stomachaches, mood swings, and difficulties in concentration.

Stage of Exhaustion. Once the body has used up all of its stored energy, its ability to withstand stress is depleted and the body enters a stage of exhaustion. The teen can no longer handle any stressors and is in grave danger of serious physical and/or mental harm.

Scientific Research on Stress

Extensive research on laboratory animals and humans has shown that stress, especially prolonged or severe stress, can interfere with normal body functions, cause disturbances in proper chemical production, affect organs, cause several different types of illness, and affect a person's social functioning.

In 1936 Selye was one of the first scientists to conclude that animals subjected to prolonged stress in the form of trauma, excessive heat or cold, electric shock, or other life-threatening assault, developed physical abnormalities including enlargement and overactivity of the adrenal cortex, shrinking of the thymus gland, irregularities in the lymph nodes, and stomach ulcers.[6] Since then numerous scientists and researchers have expanded the knowledge on stress and its association to physical, mental, and social ailments. They have been able to identify specific chemical changes that stress produces and link these changes to specific diseases.

During the 1950s Sawrey and Weisz were actually able to produce gastric ulcers in rats by exposing them to severe stress through aversion stimulation. In 1958 and 1962 H. I. Russek conducted extensive research on stress and heart disease. Through study and investigation of more than two hundred men, Russek was able to determine that prolonged stress was far more significant in the occurrence of coronary disease in young adults than hereditary conditions or diet.[7] In 1978 McCarty and Kopin documented hormone response patterns in rhesus monkeys. They showed that monkeys subjected to prolonged environmental stress (the monkey received weekly seventy-two-hour continuous shock avoidance sessions) had elevated corticosteroid levels.[8] In 1982 J. W. Mason, a noted clinical psychophysiologist, advanced the study of stress and physical illness one step further when he proved through clinical trials that individuals who showed extreme values (either higher or lower) of corticosteroid and other hormones were at greater risk of developing disease than were individuals who had moderate values.[9] Mason had made the link between stress and its effect on the body's immune system.

The effects of stress can also be measured in people's social behavior. When researchers measure how stress affects social behavior, they look for symptoms or changes in a person's physical or mental state. Scientists have observed four different types of stress symptoms in adolescents. They are the physical, emotional, mental, and behavioral symptoms. Together they are referred to as the multiple manifestations of stress, and all are linked in some way to the chemical changes that take place in the body during the General Adaptive Syndrome, or the teen's reaction to stress.[10]

Physical Symptoms of Stress

During the teen years the body is very active in the growth process. Both males and females will attain their adult height, weight, musculoskeletal and organ size between the ages of thirteen and twenty.[11] While this great surge of physical development is happening, teenagers may also be dealing with difficult stressors such as parents' expectations, school achievement, and their own sexuality. Stressors like this can activate the General Adaptive Syndrome, which will initiate hormone and chemical imbalances within the body, and cause teens to exhibit physical symptoms of stress.

Mental Symptoms of Stress

Being a teenager is confusing enough, but when stress is added to the equation teens undergo several disturbing mental symptoms that dramatically affect their ability to study, work, participate in activities, or even enjoy themselves. Many of the mental symptoms teens experience may be caused when the production of stress steroids overrides or interferes with normal hormone secretion.

Are You Under Stress?

The physical symptoms of stress include:

- change in appetite—not being hungry at appropriate times or constantly feeling hungry
- irritability—feeling cranky and uncomfortable
- constipation
- diarrhea
- dizziness—feeling light-headed when sitting or standing
- fatigue—experiencing a constant lack of energy and feeling tired throughout the day
- frequent colds
- headaches that seem to begin in the morning and last most of the day
- increased perspiration or feeling hot and sweaty in the absence of exertion
- low grade fever—running a slightly elevated temperature for several days with no other symptoms
- rashes on the face, trunk, or extremities
- sleep difficulties, such as sleeping too much, experiencing insomnia, or waking several times during the night
- stomachaches
- sore throat or feeling a constant tightness within the throat
- tense muscles
- stiff jaw or grinding teeth
- restlessness, or the inability to settle down and relax

It's Not All in Your Head

Here are some of the more common mental symptoms of stress:

☐ inability to concentrate or focus on a task

☐ difficulty in making decisions or constantly changing one's mind

☐ loss of self-confidence or ability to believe in oneself

☐ making rash decisions or taking unreasonable risks

☐ tendency to lose perspective on things

Emotional Symptoms of Stress

It is not unusual for teenagers to experience a wide range of emotions in the course of a normal day. Usually the emotional reactions are appropriate, like worrying about an upcoming test, feeling disappointed about striking out at bat, or crying during a sad part in a movie. But when teenagers are under a great deal of stress, their bodies are often in an arousal state causing their emotional reactions to escalate and become inappropriate.

Behavioral Symptoms of Stress

Teenagers under stress often experience a change or escalation in their behavior, due to the extended state of arousal of their bodies. This behavior may take the form of arguing more often with family members, dressing in punk or skinhead fashion, or

Riding an Emotional Roller Coaster

These are some typical emotional reactions teens exhibit when under significant stress:

- not caring about things that they once took an interest in

- nightmares or sleep-disrupting dreams

- excessive worrying beyond the normal concern for things

- panic or fearful feelings that disrupt their actions or activities

- feelings of failure or of inadequacy

- angry outbursts that are more frequent and more intensified

- feelings of being unworthy or of thinking that they do not deserve help or assistance or rewards

- feeling guilty about things they did or things they think they should have done

- giddiness at inappropriate times

- feeling insecure and lonely

- mood swings or the exhibition of inconsistent temperaments

- crying for no particular reason

- negative feelings or thinking nothing is worthwhile

- nervousness or feeling constantly ready to react

missing classes or days from school. Unfortunately, many times a teen's stress-related behavior may be misinterpreted as just STB (stupid teenage behavior) instead of as a symptom of stress. It is important to recognize that the following behaviors are not just STBs but rather behavior symptoms caused by teen stress.

Why Teens Experience Stress

Stress is a normal aspect of life. No one can live stress-free, but certain age groups can deal with stress better than others. Being a teenager is not easy. In today's challenging and complex society an adolescent's day can be filled with many stressful events. In addition to being faced with many developmental tasks, trying to establish one's own identity, and taking on increased responsibilities associated with approaching adulthood, teenagers are also trying to meet the demands placed upon them by family, school, and peers. Most teenagers are on the go from around six o'clock in the morning right through until ten or eleven at night, almost every day. They are accountable to their parents, their teachers, and their friends. They must be adept at working alone, in small groups, and in large groups. In a single day teenagers assume several different roles and are expected to perform adequately in each as a child, sibling, student, athlete, employee, or friend. Since each role brings with it a set of expectations, demands, and goals, teenagers are constantly being asked to measure up. It is no wonder that the teen years, in general, are filled with stress.

As a group, teenagers have a more difficult time

Is It STB or Stress?

Behavioral symptoms caused by stress include:

- alcohol and drug use, in an attempt to escape from the stress or to feel good
- accident proneness
- attention-seeking behaviors, such as outright disobedience or fighting
- changes in appearance (including weight loss or gain), appearing inappropriately dressed, or wearing the same outfit several days in a row
- fighting more frequently with relatives, friends, and strangers
- fire setting
- giving up easily or not being able to accomplish assigned tasks on a regular basis
- impulsive behavior or consistently initiating action before thinking out what you will do
- lack of interest in normal activities that should be of interest to teens your age
- skipping school on a regular basis
- stealing both things you need and want and things you do not need or want
- yelling when answering in a normal tone would be more appropriate
- nail-biting
- pulling out strands and clumps of hair
- smoking
- neglecting hygiene
- developing an eating disorder, such as anorexia or bulimia

dealing with stress because they are in transition, no longer children but not quite adults, dependent upon parents but moving toward independence. This state of transition brings with it a set of demands that the teen must deal with. Identity is one of these demands. Who is the teenager? What values has he or she established? What goals will he or she pursue? Physical development is another demand. The fourteen-year-old's body may appear to have reached full development, but growth hormones are still being activated and body organs have not reached maturity. Sexual identity is also an emerging demand during the teen years. While a fifteen-year-old's body has attained sexual functioning, the teen's ability to process and accept his or her own sexual behavior may not be solidified. Clearly this is a period of redefinition, a time when the adolescent is experimenting with ideas, relationships, and roles.

Just the state of being a teenager has its own inherent demands, and in addition teens are also vulnerable to the stressors that all people must endure, such as being late for an appointment, arguing with a friend, or experiencing a divorce within the family. It is important for teens to realize that during this critical period of transition they may not be able to navigate the transition alone. In many instances having a best friend who will listen, understand, and offer suggestions can make a big difference to a teenager. Another important fact to remember is that the teen years have a beginning and a definite ending. This period of being in between is a bridge to another age and time when the individual will have achieved self-identity, maturity, and sexual responsibility. When an adolescent is fifteen, it may

Stress-busters

Adolescence is a vulnerable period that is often characterized by life changes, personal conflicts, physical development, and other stressors. It is important for teens to

1. recognize possible stressors
2. know which stressors they can evade and which they must deal with
3. learn ways to deal with stress effectively
4. know their stress limits

If teenagers can accomplish these four important steps, they can take control of their own well-being. While no one can lead a stress-free life, every teenager can learn to manage stress and experience a more healthful, content adolescence.

appear as if the stressors are overwhelming, but in a matter of time these stressors will disappear. No one is fifteen forever!

Every teenager is exposed to stress on a daily basis and will exhibit some physical, mental, emotional, and behavioral symptoms of stress during adolescence. This is a normal process, but if symptoms are occurring frequently, interfering with daily functioning, or are strong and persistent, this is a signal that the teenager is experiencing severe stress and may need outside intervention. Help is available in many forms. Sometimes just talking over a problem with a parent or favorite teacher can give a better perspective. The school guidance department is staffed by professional counselors who can also help teens evaluate their problems, identify options, and make choices. School counselors can also direct teens to organizations or other professionals who can provide help for specific problems.

2

Types of Stress and How to Cope

T he previous chapter examined the biological ways in which the human body responds to stress, along with the multiple manifestations that teens exhibit. This chapter will look at the types of stress teens experience, and ways they can cope with stress.

Not All Types of Stress Are Equal

In general, teenagers experience three different types of stress—*major life transitions, enduring life stress,* and *chronic daily stress*—that activate the General Adaptation Syndrome. During the stress reaction the teenager's body responds the same whether the stressor is a major life transition, enduring life stress, or chronic daily stress. The only difference is the

Enduring Life Stress

Enduring life stress focuses on negative events that teenagers potentially have some control over. In general, enduring life stress focuses on concerns about academic achievements, social relationships, parental expectations, peer pressures, and future plans. Enduring life stress includes:

- arguing with parents
- being suspended from school
- breaking up with a boyfriend or girlfriend
- failing to make an athletic team or be elected to school office
- failing a course in school
- your girlfriend getting pregnant
- getting a new job
- joining a new club
- losing a job
- losing an important object
- not getting along with siblings or peers
- not getting along with a teacher

Chronic Daily Stress

Chronic daily stresses are those little things that happen almost every day that can set off a teenager or disrupt his or her routine. Some of these chronic daily stresses include:

- being late for class, work, or activity
- change in privileges or responsibilities at home
- disagreement with parents
- disagreement with brothers or sisters
- disagreement with friends
- feeling pressured by friends
- getting too much homework
- missing the school bus
- not getting enough sleep

Major Life Transitions

Major life transitions are the most serious type of stress that adolescents will experience. Teens usually do not have control over major life transitions and this type of stress usually happens quickly and unexpectedly. Often they can have long-term effects upon the teen. Major life transitions include:

- accident or illness that causes a visible deformity
- addition of a third adult to the family
- becoming pregnant
- beginning or changing to a new school
- birth or adoption of a brother or sister
- brother or sister leaving home
- change in financial status of the family
- death of a parent, brother, or sister
- death of a close relative
- death of a childhood friend
- divorce or separation of parents
- discovery of being adopted
- hospitalization of a parent, brother, or sister
- incarceration of parent, brother, or sister in jail
- parent's loss of job
- marriage of a parent to a stepparent
- moving to a new community
- natural disasters affecting communities, such as flood, hurricane, tornado, fire
- pregnancy of an unwed sister
- repeating a grade in school

intensity and duration of the stress reaction. In most cases, major life transitions are the most serious kinds of demands placed upon teenagers, while chronic daily stress is the least serious. When a teen experiences a major life transition, the alarm stage of the General Adaptation Syndrome is more intense and the resistance stage is longer than if he or she were experiencing chronic daily stress.

It is important to remember that all three types of stress produce wear and tear on a teen's body, and that a year filled with enduring life stress can cause just as much body damage as one major life stress. Stress is cumulative; every time the body initiates the General Adaptation Syndrome it adds up! Knowing what type of stress is present in your life is the first step toward managing stress.

Stress is produced by both big demands and small demands. It comes from the interactions teens have with their environment and with their friends, family, coworkers, authority figures, and enemies. It also comes from the goals teens have set for themselves. There are stress experiences over which teens have no control and stress experiences that teens can easily avoid by modifying or changing how they do something. Stress is a multidimensional aspect within a teen's life, yet it does not have to dominate a teen's life. By learning about the different types of stress and developing proper coping strategies, teens can reduce the amount of stress in their lives.

Coping With Stress

While stress may be an ever-present aspect of life, it does not have to cause an unlimited amount of discomfort. Instead teens can do something to avoid some of the pain stress causes. This is called coping, which is "simply defined as the things individuals do to avoid being harmed by life strains."[1] In the early 1980s several social scientists working independently made three important discoveries about the way humans cope with stress. Rudolph Moos and Andrew Billings looked at all the ways people cope with stress and classified them into three categories based upon how a person thought, expressed, or acted upon the stress experience. Coping strategies that were based upon how a person thought about a stress experience were called *cognitive coping strategies*. Coping strategies that demonstrated how a person expressed his or her stress were called *emotional coping strategies*. Coping strategies that incorporated direct action were labeled *practical coping strategies.*[2]

Cognitive coping strategies are methods that help a person think of the stressful experience as being not as bad as they originally thought it was. Typical cognitive coping strategies include

- accepting the experience and recognizing what can and cannot be done to change it

- concentrating on the good things that might come out of the situation

- not allowing themselves to dwell on the stressful experience and lose focus on other aspects of their life.

Emotional coping strategies are methods that show how a person expresses, suppresses, or counteracts the negative feelings about the experience. Typical emotional coping strategies include

- trying to blame others for the source of the stress

- abusing substances like drugs and alcohol in an effort to forget about the stress

- denying that the experience was stressful or that the stress has an effect upon them

Practical coping strategies are ways in which a person actively tries to find a solution to the problem causing the stress. Typical practical strategies include

- seeking advice from others on ways to deal with the stressful experience

- finding out more information so that they can solve the problem

- trying to change or alter the experience

Hoffman, Levy-Shiff, Sohlberg, and Zarizki, also working on stress and coping research, found that teenagers who had a significant knowledge about stress and coping strategies, in general, were more likely to choose coping strategies that were more effective.[3] Roy Cameron and Don Meichenbaum took all this research one step further and actually developed a framework, or model, for effective coping.[4] Their model is based upon four stages. In order for a person to complete each stage of the model, he or she must have specific knowledge about stress and coping strategies. In addition, a person must complete all four stages in order for the model to be successful.

The steps for coping with stress may sound a bit complicated, but Cameron and Meichenbaum's model on the next page is actually quite simple and effective. The major function that takes place in *step 1* is to analyze the problem from an objective point of view.

A Model for Coping With Stress

1. *A person must make an accurate appraisal or interpretation of the stress experience.*
   a) His or her interpretation must be valid.
   b) This interpretation must be supported by facts and opinions of people knowledgeable enough to make a judgment.
   c) This interpretation should be free of any personal bias or distortion.

2. *A person must have an adequate knowledge of all forms of cognitive, emotional, and practical coping strategies.*
   a) He or she must be able to accurately evaluate all the coping strategies in relationship to the specific stressful event.
   b) He or she must select the proper combinations of coping strategies to use.

3. *A person must be willing to use the appropriate coping strategies.*
   a) He or she must have the ability to activate the approriate coping strategies.
   b) He or she must have the body energy necessary to activate the appropriate coping strategies.

4. *A person's body must return to a normal rate or pattern of psychological and biological functioning.*

A teenager can talk to a friend, parent, or favorite teacher and tell them what happened and get feedback on how they interpret the event. Because these people are not involved in the actual problem, their interpretation can be objective. With input from these knowledgeable and objective sources, a teen can evaluate if his or her interpretation is valid. If it is, then the teenager knows he or she has analyzed the problem objectively. But if the teen's interpretation is different, perhaps the teenager needs to reconsider his or her initial feelings and rethink what actually happened.

The major function that takes place in *step 2* is to bring to mind all the possible coping strategies that an adolescent knows of and then make a decision on which ones to use. At this point a teenager should do some brainstorming. He or she can make contact with other teens who may have experienced a similar problem and ask them how they dealt with it. Or the adolescent can talk with a guidance counselor or other adult who can suggest some coping strategies to be used. A teenager can also think about similar incidents he or she has experienced in the past and consider what coping strategies were successful then. It is important to keep in mind that Hoffman, Levy-Shiff, Sohlberg, and Zarizki found that teenagers who had a broad knowledge of stress and coping strategies were more likely to choose coping strategies that were most effective.

In *step 3* a teenager will activate the appropriate coping strategies he or she chooses from the work done in steps 1 and 2, keeping in mind that a combination of strategies is necessary to attain relief. When a stressful event happens, it affects a person's physical and mental being and therefore the most successful coping strategies will center on relieving the negative effects on both a person's mind and body.

The *final step* in the Cameron and Meichenbaum model focuses on actually feeling relief both mentally and physically from the stress event. Very simply, if the teenager feels better, then the coping strategies chosen have worked.

This may sound like a big procedure, and teens using this model for the first time may be uncomfortable, but, like learning how to inline skate or drive a car, the more they practice the method, the better they become at using it. Dealing with stress is not as simple as choosing one coping strategy and using it every time a teen experiences stress. No one can effectively put aside a stressful event or chase it away with drugs or alcohol, but it is possible for teens to learn how to develop the right coping strategies and how to activate these coping strategies. Unfortunately, many teens have not been adequately educated about stress and coping strategies and choose to withdraw from or deny the existence of stress within their lives. Teens who recognize stress, put it in perspective, and actively deal with it will suffer less serious effects of stress than teens who through ignorance or choice let stress disrupt their lives.

3

Major Life Transitions

The most difficult type of stress for teens to deal with is one within the *major life transition* category. In addition to causing intense levels of stress, major life transitions may also have long-term emotional and psychological effects upon adolescents. Major life transitions are like earthquakes that register seven or above on the Richter scale. They can hit teens without warning, shake them up, and cause major disruptions within their lives. They are serious threats to an individual's well-being, and often they can cause drastic changes and effects that will require a long recovery. When a teen experiences a major life transition, his or her body is at risk for depleting the energy needed to deal with additional stress. His or her mind may be too unclear to choose appropriate coping strategies, causing the development of many of the physical, emotional, mental, and behavioral symptoms of stress overload.

It is important to understand that in most cases teenagers have little or no control over major life transitions. They cannot control whether or not their parents will get a divorce or lose their jobs or if a family member will die. The stress teens experience from major life transitions can be catastrophic if appropriate interventions are not available. Let's take a look at how some young people have been affected by major life stresses.

Danny

Danny was a ninth grader. This was his first year at Midway High School. Like other freshmen getting used to a new school, making new friends and adjusting to a new school routine was not easy. He did satisfactory work at the middle school and finished the eighth grade with a *C* average. He was looking forward to going to high school so he could ride to school with his older brother Jimmy who was a junior there. But early in the school year Jimmy was arrested for stealing cars. Because it was not his first offense, he was sent to the Youth Correctional Institution. For Danny, his brother's arrest was a major life transition, although he was not aware of it.

Danny's parents always seemed to be fighting now over what to do about Jimmy. His mother blamed his father for working too much and not paying enough attention to Jimmy, for not being a real father to their son. Danny's father blamed his mother for always covering up for Jimmy's mistakes, babying him, and making excuses for his behavior. Danny missed his brother, and he worried about his being in prison. He hated being the only kid in the house because now his parents made him do all the things Jimmy used to do around the house. They also criticized Danny and found fault with lots of things he did. When Danny got in trouble for being out too late one night, his father accused him of being just like Jimmy.

At school some of the new kids Danny was just getting to know began to avoid him. He heard that their parents didn't want them to hang around with Danny because he might be into the same sort of things that caused Jimmy to be arrested. Once when he talked back to one of his teachers who was questioning him about being absent from school for a few days, the teacher shook his head and said, "Sounds like you're on your way to end up just like your brother, in jail."

By the middle of the school year, Danny was overwhelmed. He was swamped by schoolwork, and he couldn't concentrate in class. He was always tired, probably because he had trouble falling asleep at night. In addition, when he did fall asleep, sometimes he had bad dreams that woke him up. He was not getting along with his parents, and lately he had started to yell back at them when they yelled at him. He would skip school at least once a week and call himself in sick after his parents left for work. It just seemed as if Danny's world had turned upside down since his brother went to jail.

Ellen

Ellen had just turned fifteen when her parents told her and her two younger sisters that they had decided to get a divorce. This was a major life transition for Ellen.

The next week her dad packed up his things and moved into an apartment across town. Since Ellen was the oldest, her mother confided in her and told Ellen that her father had been having an affair with another woman for the last four years. Ellen did not know how to deal with this information. She still loved her dad but was confused by the anger she now felt toward him. Ellen knew that her mother was hurt and angry, but she didn't know how to reply, especially when her mother would say bad things about her father.

Ellen had a close friend named Lisa whom she had been friends with since third grade. Ellen told Lisa about her parents but made her promise not to tell any of their friends. At first it seemed easy for Ellen to adjust to her parents' separation and hide the truth about her parents' breakup, but when her mother told her that she would be going back to work, life got a little bit more uncomfortable. Ellen's mother was a nurse practitioner, and she would now be working the 4:00 P.M. to midnight shift at the Trauma Center of University Hospital. This meant that Ellen would be responsible for her sisters after school and throughout the evening.

Ellen began spending less time with her friends because she usually had to be home from school by 3:30 P.M. so her mother could leave for her job. Soon she drifted away from her old circle of friends and began to share less things about her life with her mother. She met some different kids at school. Without her mother knowing, Ellen's new friends would come over to her house two or three times a week at about 9:30 in the evening, just to hang around. By then Ellen had sent her younger sisters off to bed, and the kids had the house to themselves. Ellen started to dress differently. Instead of her usual jeans, shirt, and sneakers, she liked to dress all in black. She went down to the Army-Navy surplus store and bought a pair of black leather lace-up boots and shoplifted a couple of pairs of black socks. Since her new friends smoked, Ellen started to smoke. When they started to bring beer over, Ellen began to drink. After a while, she was smoking marijuana. Sometimes she would feel so bad about lying to her mother that she would try to be extra nice to her. And then at other times she was so angry at her mother for working and being away so much that she screamed at her, "I hate you, I hate you!" In order to pay for her cigarettes and to chip in for the beer and marijuana, Ellen often would steal five or ten dollars from her mother's wallet and sometimes from the pocketbooks of other students when they left them out at school. For Ellen, stealing had become no big deal.

Steve

The summer between tenth and eleventh grade Steve's father was in and out of the hospital due to illness. Toward the end of July he was diagnosed with cancer. For Steve this was a major life transition. Steve, his older sister Pam, and younger sister Linda were told about their father's illness. Together, they spoke openly about how their dad's illness would affect the family. Steve and his sisters talked with the doctors, visited their father daily, and anxiously awaited his discharge from the hospital. His dad's diagnosis was very positive, and with chemotherapy and radiation there was an 85 percent chance that he would be cured.

But even with such a favorable prognosis, Steve worried constantly.

In September Pam left home to attend college, Linda began high school, and Steve entered his junior year. Shortly after, Steve's dad resumed his job on a part-time basis while undergoing cancer treatments. Steve was an accomplished athlete; he had been on the varsity soccer and baseball teams, but this year he decided not to try out. Although his grades were good both freshman and sophomore years (he had a *B* average), he told his coach that he needed more time to study and couldn't do that if he played a sport.

As fall continued, Steve did not join any of the school activities he had participated in the year before. Instead he spent most of his time studying by himself or doing things alone in his room. He was not happy now if he only got a *B* or *B-plus*. He *had* to get an *A*. He let his hair grow long and was usually seen during his spare time listening to hard rock music on his Walkman.

At home he was more quiet than usual and often complained of feeling tired, having a sore throat, and never being hungry. He lost about fifteen pounds. His mother noticed that Steve seemed to be overly concerned about things. He frequently asked her if the family had enough money. And every time anyone bought clothes, suggested the family go out to dinner, or spoke about purchasing something, Steve would always say, "Are you sure we have enough money for that?" At school he was on his way to becoming a straight *A* student. His homework was always on time, correct, and neat. His school projects were outstanding and he had asked his guidance counselor if he could take an additional subject second semester. But he had no friends or social activities. In addition, Steve never felt as if he were doing well enough academically. He told his younger sister often that he felt so bad because he just wasn't good enough.

Sara

Sara was at school one morning when the principal entered her math class and asked to speak to her. This was unusual, and Sara had a feeling that something was wrong. When Sara walked into the principal's office, she saw that her guidance counselor was already there. The counselor told Sara that her father had been involved in a car accident and was at Memorial Hospital. She would take Sara over there immediately.

When Sara arrived at the hospital, her mother tearfully told her that her father had died in the accident. The news hit Sara hard. Although she didn't know it, she was embarking on a major life transition. Sara immediately felt dizzy and thought she was going to throw up. Then she started to cry, and it seemed as if she cried all day. That night she and her mother stayed up almost all night talking about her father, crying sometimes and laughing other times when they talked about his doing his usual funny things.

The next few days were very difficult for Sara. People kept stopping by to say they were sorry her dad had died. She was trying to help her mom make funeral arrangements, and there were so many things that had to get done. After the funeral Sara and her mom tried to get their life back to normal. Sara was not ready to go right back to school. She felt tired and drained. Her mom arranged for her to stay home for another week. Together they used that time to get used to being a family of two. They talked about their feelings and their plans. When Sara returned to school, she was more rested.

At first it was difficult to get back to her studies, but each day she tried to do a little more than the day before. Sometimes her days were manageable, and other times she would feel lonely and sad. When she felt down, she tried not to be alone. She would call up a friend or talk to her mother. She also went to the library and got several books that were written for teenagers about losing a parent. After reading them she realized that her feelings of sadness were normal. As time passed, Sara adjusted to being without her father. That semester some of her grades dropped, but she didn't flunk anything and she knew that she was doing the best she could under the circumstances.

Choosing Coping Strategies

Danny, Ellen, Steve, and Sara are living with a high degree of stress due to a particular major life transition. But each reacted differently. What made Danny act out in response to his stress while Steve threw himself into his studies? How come Ellen began to use marijuana while Sara didn't? The answers to these questions center around the choice of coping strategies Danny, Ellen, Steve, and Sara used to try to avoid the harm from the major life transition each experienced.

No single coping strategy is totally effective or guarantees a positive outcome. Choosing the right combination of coping strategies will play an important role in how successful a teen will be in avoiding harm from the stress in his or her life. Let's review the coping strategies discussed in the previous chapter. Cognitive coping strategies are based on how a person thinks about the stress experience. Emotional coping strategies are ways in which people express, deny, or counteract the negative feelings of the stress experience. Practical coping strategies are the direct actions people take to change the stress experience.

Who Coped the Best with Stress?

Now, let's take another look at Danny, Ellen, Steve, and Sara. Go back and read the vignettes again. This time take a piece of paper and try to answer the following questions without reading any further in this chapter. (Do not write in this book.)

1. What were the major life transitions experienced by Danny, Ellen, Steve, and Sara?
2. What were the physical, emotional, and behavioral symptoms that indicated that these teenagers were experiencing stress overload?
3. What coping strategies did each teen use?
4. Which teen was able to manage his or her stress the most successfully?
5. How would you have handled the major life transitions if they happened to you?

Now let's read on and analyze what is going on in the lives of Danny, Ellen, Steve, and Sara so you can see how you did.

Stress Double Whammy Floors Danny. As a first year student at a new high school, Danny must cope with getting used to a whole new educational environment, including new friends and a new schedule. In addition to this major life transition, Danny's brother has been put in jail. So now Danny is faced with two major life transitions. It appears as if Danny is exhibiting a variety of stress symptoms. Physically, he is having some difficulties getting to sleep and sleeping through the night. Mentally, his stress symptoms are being expressed through his inability to concentrate on his schoolwork and focus on tasks. Emotionally, Danny is exhibiting angry outbursts and is subject to nightmares. Danny's behavioral symptoms include arguing more with his parents and skipping school. Danny feels overwhelmed, and perhaps this is why he is unable to initiate effective coping strategies and manage his stress.

First, Danny must realize that he is experiencing two major life transitions and accept the fact that he is not responsible for these stress events, nor can he stop them from happening. Danny would be wise to talk with his guidance counselor at school about how he feels and what is going on in his life. His counselor could provide some suggestions on how Danny could cope with the stress he is under. The counselor could also put Danny in contact with other students whose siblings have recently left home. In addition, the counselor may speak with Danny's parents so that they can be informed about how Danny is being affected by the stress and perhaps give them some suggestions about dealing more appropriately with Danny.

Escapism Increases Ellen's Stress Level. Divorce is a major transition for any teenager, and Ellen seems to be having a difficult time adjusting to it. Her desire to escape from the stress and new responsibilities placed upon her because of the divorce is her way of using emotional coping strategies, such as smoking marijuana and drinking beer, to lessen the pain. But it is not working, and her new behaviors could lead to even more stressful events. Ellen will be more successful if she initiates cognitive coping strategies, such as accepting the fact that her parents are getting a divorce, and channels her energy into finding ways to make the best of the experience. This will help her move beyond the pain. In addition, Ellen can implement some practical coping strategies, such as talking things over with her mother, joining a school or church group for children of divorced parents, or just reaching out to her old friend, in order to receive the support she needs to deal with this stress.

Denial Does in Steve. Steve, like Ellen and Danny, tried to deal with the major life transition he was experiencing by turning inward and moving away from those who could help him. It was as if he was trying to deny that anything was wrong within his family, yet his constant worrying, fatigue, weight loss, and sore throats were typical mental, physical, emotional, and behavioral signs of stress overload. While his use of emotional coping strategies did not yield negative behavior, such as substance abuse or stealing, his effort to deny his stress was exhibited in his almost obsessive focus on getting good grades. And even though being a good student may be a positive goal, Steve was not able to feel good about it, and he gave up a very healthy and important aspect of life (sports and friendships) in order to become a better student.

Sara Copes with Stress. Sara also experienced a major life transition, but unlike the other students Sara was more successful at dealing with her stress. She did not try to deny her pain or hold back her feelings. She cried and she sought help from her mother. She talked about her feelings a lot, and this made it seem a little easier for her to keep her father's death from interfering with the practical things she and her mother had to do. Sara experienced many physical signs of stress overload. She was tired, fatigued, and not ready to go back to school. That extra week at home renewed her physical energy so that she was able to initiate cognitive and practical coping strategies. These strategies included working with her mother on ways they could help each other accept the loss of Sara's father and explore the many changes that were now going to happen within their lives. When she did return to school, Sara concentrated on making each day a little better than the one before it. She knew it was not going to be easy, but with the energy she had regained and the way she was approaching her father's death, she was able to effectively use coping strategies to lessen the negative aspects of stress.

Risk of Stress Overload

When teens experience major life transitions, the level and the intensity of stress they are subjected to are overwhelming. In most cases it is almost impossible for teens to deal effectively with this type of stress solely by themselves. They need to look beyond their own coping mechanisms and seek professional help. Almost all school systems employ counseling professionals who can provide assistance to students. School guidance counselors plan and deliver programs and counseling services that match the needs of the psychosocial development of adolescents. School guidance programs include confidential counseling, crisis intervention, and skill development workshops. School counselors are also a reliable source of information for students. Counselors are knowledgeable about school and community resources including self-help groups like Alanon, child advocate services provided by the local county or state, and community facilities and agencies that offer programs for teens. The school guidance counselor can offer emotional support and intervention for teens experiencing stress. They are resources that adolescents can turn to for problems that exist both in and out of school.

In addition, many community organizations and agencies offer outreach assistance. A comprehensive listing of local resources can usually be found in the yellow pages of the telephone book under headings such as Alcohol Information and Treatment, Counselors, and Hospitals. School counselors, principals, and youth coordinators at the local YMCA or teen center also may have local social service directories that list community resources.

It is important to realize that any teenager who experiences a major life transition can be at risk for serious stress overload and may need professional counseling or other type of intervention.

4

Enduring Life Stress

The second category of stress that teens experience is called *enduring life stress*. For some teenagers, this type of stress seems to be as frequent, troublesome, and complex as math homework. That is because adolescence is a transitional period in which children are developing into self-sufficient adults, and this process of change can be very stressful. Some common experiences young people undergo during adolescence include demands for personal recognition, struggles for independence and identity, increasing peer pressure, concern with self-image, understanding their own sexuality, uncertainty about the future, inadequate finances, parental expectations, and academic success. These are typical events that can cause enduring life stress.

While some teenagers may progress through adolescence without ever experiencing a major life transition, many teenagers will experience frequent episodes of enduring life stress. That's because this type of stress comes from interactions teens have with their family, friends, school, work, and activities. Most enduring life stress faced by teens centers around four specific areas that include concerns about academic achievement, pressure to establish and maintain social relationships, relationships with the family, and concern for one's future. Let's take a look at each one of these areas more closely.

School Pressure

School plays a major role in a teen's life. During a typical school day, most teens will spend eight to ten hours preparing for and attending classes and school activities. There is a lot of pressure on teens to succeed academically. This pressure is internal, coming from the students themselves, and external, coming from teachers and parents.

During a school day, most teens will attend six classes and interface with six different teachers who try to direct and guide an adolescent's academic accomplishments. While in class, teens are simultaneously acquiring knowledge and skills, attaining performance-based goals, and meeting the academic expectations of their parents. Teens also must learn to balance a full school day with after-school activities and perhaps a part-time job. That's a lot of pressure! It is no wonder that the teen years are filled with many academic stresses.

School Stress

Typical academic stresses for teens include:

- ❑ choosing the right courses in junior and senior high school

- ❑ understanding the material being taught in classes

- ❑ keeping up with the required schoolwork

- ❑ maintaining satisfactory or good grades in all courses

- ❑ balancing a part-time job, school assignments, and other activities

Social Relationships

Social relationships play another important role in an adolescent's environment and development. Very few teenagers are free of peer influences, pressures, and judgments. While at school, teens interact with several hundred peers, peers who may either share or have conflicting behaviors, opinions, and goals. Teens are also acquiring skills necessary to deal with people and experiences in new environments.

During the teen years, young men and women are learning how to navigate similar and conflicting attitudes, when to assert themselves among friends, and when to make compromises. It is a period of change, a period of experimentation, and a period of adjustment.

Social Stress

Typical social relationships that can cause stress include:

- ☐ making friends
- ☐ choosing which activities, clubs, and organizations to join
- ☐ conforming to group norms for dress, language, and leisure activities
- ☐ dating
- ☐ coming to terms with one's sexuality

Family Pressures

Family relationships usually become strained during the adolescent years. Teens no longer see their parents as the center of their lives. They are able to do more things on their own and want to distance themselves from the protection and guidance their parents provide. Teens are eager to experiment with newfound freedom and want to be noticed as individuals and taken seriously as they move from childhood dependency into adult independence. In addition adolescents demand privacy, which is vastly different from the companionship they needed as infants and children. In their desire to become independent, teens often appear self-centered and egotistical around their family members, but this is only one of several roles teens are trying on in their quest for adulthood.

Family Stress

Some typical family relationship stresses include:

☐ getting along with parents and/or stepparents

☐ getting along with siblings

☐ conforming to parental expectation

☐ accepting house rules, such as curfews, chores, or limited use of telephone and car

Life Achievement Pressures

In addition to tangible stressors, such as academics, peer pressure, and family expectations, today's teenagers are facing an uncertain future. Technology, the increased cost of living, medical discoveries, population changes, international alliances, and other aspects of the twentieth-century way of life are affecting the future opportunities and choices that teens will have. Today, many families need two incomes just to make ends meet, and economists are predicting that foreign labor and technology will eliminate many types of jobs in the next decade. The cost of a college education has skyrocketed, and in many families, if teens want to continue their education after completing high school, they have to work while in high school in order to pay for it.

In addition, America's intervention in foreign disputes and wars has changed the peacetime army into a "lean, mean war machine." The American dream, which included a career, marriage, family, and a home, is no longer everyone's choice nor is it available to every American.

Life Stress

Typical future concerns that can be stressful for teens include:

- ❑ choosing a career or deciding what to major in at college

- ❑ finding the right school, college, or university

- ❑ registering for the draft

- ❑ having to leave home

Teens Can Control Certain Stresses

Although these stressors are not earth shaking, they can be difficult to deal with. In general, they should not cause serious risk to an adolescent's well-being if handled properly. It is important to realize that most of the events within the enduring life stress category can be affected by behavior and intervention. Teenagers have some control over enduring life stress, and they can affect the outcome. It may require a change in behavior or attitude or developing a new skill, but teens can reduce their amount of enduring life stress.

Another aspect of enduring life stress is that the coping strategies necessary to deal with this type of stress can easily be learned and used. Because of these two important characteristics, enduring life stress does not have to have a devastating effect upon teens.

However, it will pose a serious threat to an adolescent's health and well-being if the teen faces an ongoing series of enduring life stresses that continue over a long period of time. Stress is cumulative. The more stress that teenagers have, the more their bodies will be negatively affected and the closer they will get to exhaustion. Let's look at how other young people have been affected by enduring life stresses.

Sandy

Sandy woke up early and quickly got ready for school. She was anxious to get there to see if she had made the junior varsity cheering squad. For the past two weeks she had stayed after school every day to practice, and she hoped it would pay off. She heard her mother in the kitchen getting ready for work. Sandy wanted to make it out the door before her mother saw her because she wasn't in the mood to talk right now. As she came down the stairs quietly, she heard her mother call out, "Sandy? Sandy, come here. I just want to wish you good luck. I really hope you make the team, but if you don't I do not want you to be discouraged. You can always try again next year."

For Sandy there was no next year. She wanted to make the cheering squad this year. She looked at her mom and said, "You just don't understand. I just have to make it this year. I just have to!" She picked up her books and ran out the door.

At the bus stop she couldn't think of anything else but making the cheering squad. She mentally went over yesterday's tryouts and visualized each participant's performance. She was sure she was better than Kim and Patty and Jane, but she knew that Ann and

Ginger were much better than she. She fumbled in her backpack and found her cigarettes. As Sandy lit up, she kept thinking, "I've just got to make it!" She finished her cigarette just as the bus pulled up to the curb. She got on the bus and dove for the first empty seat she saw. She did not look around to see where her friends were sitting because she didn't want to talk to anyone this morning. She just wanted to get to school, go to the gym bulletin board, and see her name on the list of junior varsity cheerleaders.

When the bus arrived at school, she was one of the first kids off. She rushed into the school, dashed past her locker, and headed straight toward the gym. As she got closer to the gym, she realized that she was clenching her jaw. She saw the crowd of girls by the bulletin board. As she approached, she felt hot and sweaty. She tried to ease her way closer to the board so that she could read the names. As she did, she bumped a girl's shoulder. It was Karen, one of the other first-year students who also tried out for the squad. "Oh, sorry," she said to Karen. "I didn't mean to bump you." She got closer to the board and looked for her name. She looked and looked and looked, but her name wasn't there. She turned away and walked back toward her locker. She could feel the tears welling up in her eyes. She kept her head down and walked past her locker and headed for the nurse's office.

She told the nurse she had a terrible headache and wanted to lie down. She just couldn't go to class, not today. While she was lying in the nurse's office, she couldn't help feeling upset. She kept thinking about what a failure she was. She dreaded the ride home on the bus because Barbara would be there telling everyone how she had made the cheering squad. And she didn't want to have to face her mother and hear her say, "Don't feel so bad; it's only a sports team. Anyway, you can try again next year." She just didn't want to hear any of it.

Sandy had invested a lot of her time, effort, and emotion into trying to get selected for the school cheerleading squad. She set her goals high and worked hard to achieve them. Her body was probably in the stage of resistance for the past two weeks. Her headache, loss of self-confidence, feelings of failure, and loss of perspective are all symptoms of the stress she is experiencing. Unfortunately, when she did not make the cheerleading squad, her response was to separate herself from others and to pretend that she was sick. By doing this, she was trying to use emotional coping strategies to deal with her stress. If Sandy is going to diminish the stress she is under, she needs to put the event in perspective and reevaluate her interpretation. Perhaps if Sandy talks with a close friend or special teacher, she will come to realize that other goals in her life may be more important than this one. She has the right to feel upset; after all she did work very hard to make the team, but she should not let this disappointment upset her as much as it has. Sandy needs to accept her disappointment and reestablish a new goal.

Eric

Eric came bounding down the stairs and stomped into the living room. He went up to his mother and started to yell, "You tell her to stay out of my room. I'm sick and tired of her coming into my room and taking out whatever she needs. She can't play my CDs. They're mine, not hers. If you don't do something about it, I'm going to hit her." By now Eric was red with anger, and his mother tried to calm him down. "Eric, she only borrowed your Grateful Dead CD. She's not going to break it. She just wants to listen to it while she's baby-sitting." But hearing this didn't help. "You always stick up for her. You let her do anything she wants. It's not fair. I don't go into her room. If I dared, she'd kill me, and you'd let her!"

Eric angrily turned away. He stomped upstairs, threw open his sister's bedroom door, and began to frantically look around for his possessions. He opened her closet and went through her things taking back one of his concert T-shirts. He could feel his hands shaking as he continued to look for his things. His head was filled with disjointed thoughts. He didn't care what his mother or sister thought. He was going to get back all his things.

At first he was somewhat careful about going through his sister's room, but once he found his T-shirt his anxiety increased and he moved more quickly from bookcase to CD player to desk. He heard his mother coming upstairs and for a second he froze. He felt anger, remorse, hatred, sadness all at once. He saw his mother standing there and before she could say a word, Eric yelled, "I hate her, I hate her." He pushed his mother aside and ran into his room slamming and locking the door. He threw himself on his bed. His head was pounding, and his throat felt as if he had swallowed a rock.

Eric's stress focuses on his relationship with his sister and has probably been going on for a long time. His stress symptoms include angry outbursts, making rash decisions, yelling, and shaking movements in his hands. He is not accepting responsibility for his part in this stressful situation but instead seems to be placing all the blame upon his sister. This type of emotional coping strategy will not help the situation. In addition, Eric's angry outbursts are only intensifying the stress.

Eric needs to look at his relationship with his sister more objectively, investigate ways in which he can channel his anger more productively, and find constructive ways to deal with his sister. Perhaps when he feels himself becoming upset and angry he should pick up his basketball and shoot hoops or take a long walk. Eric should try to talk things over with his sister when he is not so emotionally charged up, explaining to her why it is important for her to ask before she borrows anything. The two also need to address with each other their need for privacy and set some ground rules about entering each other's room. Using more practical and cognitive strategies like these will be much more successful than acting in anger.

David

David stood in the principal's office, biting his nails. His stomach hurt and was making odd noises. He paced up and down waiting for Mr. Thompson to come in. This was the third time David had been caught smoking on school property. No detention for him this time. He was going to be suspended for two days. He kept asking himself how he could have been so stupid to get caught again. What was he going to tell his folks? Boy, they were going to be really angry with him.

Just then Mr. Thompson entered the room. David felt hot and sweaty. "So, David, this is your third time smoking on school property. You know what that means." "Yes, I guess I'm suspended for a couple of days." "Yes, you are. I'll be calling your parents this afternoon to inform them.

But before I do, I'd like to give you a little advice. It's always better if the student tells the parents first, before they hear it from me. So, I recommend that you either call your mom or dad before the end of school or tell one of them as soon as you get home. I'll be calling them around 5:00 today. Your suspension will take place on Wednesday and Thursday. You are expected to go to all your classes tomorrow and after each class tell your teacher that you won't be in class Wednesday and Thursday. Listen, David, you can't smoke on school property. Besides, smoking is not good for you. If you have an addiction to nicotine, you better deal with it now before it causes you real harm. And remember, David, you cannot disobey school rules and expect to get away with it. You better go back to class now. I'll see you tomorrow."

David left the office feeling a little queasy. He knew he had to tell his folks when he got home, but it wasn't going to be easy. His mother would make him feel guilty, and his father would yell at him about acting stupid. He really didn't want to listen to them, but he had no choice. He went back to class and evaded his friends. After school he tried to act natural on the bus. He told his friends it was no big deal, so what if he got suspended. He tried to laugh and joke about it with his friends, but he was upset and a little afraid of what his parents would do.

By the time he got home he felt tired and had a headache. He sat in the living room and waited for his mother to come home from work. As soon as she came home, David told her. He said, "Look, Mom, I got into some trouble today at school. I got caught smoking, and Mr. Thompson suspended me for two days." He had told her, and it wasn't so bad. Now she would tell his dad. They would probably ground him for a month. David talked with his mother. She was angry because he was suspended and angry that he smoked. No one in their family smoked, and she just couldn't understand how David had started. While his mother talked, David listened. He really didn't want to but knew that he would only get into more trouble if he mouthed off at her. Some of the things she said were true, such as he shouldn't have taken the chance and smoked on school property. But some of the things she said were way off base, such as just because some of his friends smoked that didn't mean he had to smoke and maybe he should look for other friends. By the time she finished yelling and talking, David knew the worst was over. He actually felt better now that it was over.

David dealt with his stressful event differently than Sandy and Eric. His stress was short-term, lasting less than a day, but like Sandy and Eric, he exhibited stress symptoms including restlessness, feeling fatigued, and having a headache. David followed the Cameron and Meichenbaum's model for coping with stress outlined in Chapter 2. He interpreted his stress event accurately (being suspended from school for the first time). He had knowledge of several coping strategies and initiated them. He tried to laugh and joke about it with his friends, he listened to the advice given to him by the principal and his mother, and he was ready to accept the consequences. Through the use of these emotional, practical, and cognitive coping strategies, David was able to diminish his stress.

Patty

Patty had attended the required assembly for all juniors. The guidance staff at her high school talked about the college selection process, taking the SATs, looking up colleges in the College Guide, attending the local college fair, and visiting several colleges. However, after the assembly she felt overwhelmed. She had no idea about which college she could afford or which college would admit her. She wanted to go to college but could not imagine how her family would pay for it. After school she talked with her friends as they walked home from school. "No way I'm going to college," Laurie said. "I can barely make it through high school. I'm going to work. Maybe I'll take some computer courses at night, but I just want to get a job, make some money, and move out of my house." Most of her friends felt this way, and Patty was a little apprehensive when she said, "I want to go to college. I don't know where I can get in, or even what I want to study, but I know that if I go to college, I can do better." As she spoke, she realized how nervous she was. Her voice was a little shaky and her palms were sweaty.

When Patty got home, she looked over the SAT booklet that was handed out during the assembly. She wondered if she would be able to convince her parents that she really wanted to go to college. Would they understand? Where would she get the money? How would she find out about the different colleges? What did she have to do to apply? Her head swirled and her stomach was turning flips.

That evening she tried to talk with her parents about college, but they did not understand. Her father said that she should just finish high school and get a job. Besides it wasn't important for her to get an education. This conversation with her parents only made things more difficult. She felt guilty for wanting to go to college and angry at her parents for not understanding her needs. She decided to take a walk and clear her mind before she started her homework.

The next day she went to see her guidance counselor, Mrs. Anastos. Just before the meeting, Patty almost canceled. Would her counselor think she was stupid? She tried to collect her thoughts, but when she went in to see her guidance counselor, she just sort of fell apart. She could feel her heart racing, and she just couldn't sit still. She couldn't concentrate and forgot all the questions she wanted to ask. She felt her face turning red and thought that maybe her father was right and she should not even think about going to college. But her guidance counselor was very understanding, and told Patty that she was there to help her through the process. Mrs. Anastos explained that she would recommend some books for Patty to read and suggested that she take a career inventory to see what areas she was strongest in.

After meeting with her guidance counselor, Patty felt a little better but still realized that there were a lot of hurdles to clear if she was going to apply to college. She wanted to attend college and realized that it would be a difficult goal to achieve but not one that was beyond her reach. She knew she could not do it alone and was encouraged by the support and information her guidance counselor could supply.

Patty's stress event will be ongoing and probably will last a year or more, or until she is accepted into college. She is dealing with it in a positive manner although she is also exhibiting stress symptoms, including nervousness and the inability to concentrate. But they are not severe, and they are not interfering with her usual activities. Like David, Patty has initiated Cameron and Meichenbaum's coping model and will probably continue to use it throughout this experience with stress. She realistically evaluated the stress event, recognized what she could and could not do about it, sought out assistance from her guidance counselor, and began to find a way to solve her problem.

Angela

It was after midnight when Angela came home from her date with Ed. Angela's mother had already gone to bed, and Angela was glad not to face the usual questions her mother always asked about her dates. She put out the lights and went to her bedroom, but instead of getting ready for bed, Angela just sat on her bed thinking about what happened on her date.

Angela was only a freshman, and she had been thrilled when Ed, a senior, asked her out. This was their fourth date, and Angela really liked Ed. He was older, had his own car, and hung around with all the popular seniors. Angela couldn't believe that he was really dating her! And she would do almost anything to continue the relationship. Tonight, after the basketball game, they went over to a friend's house. There were only three couples there, and after talking for a while, Ed took Angie's hand and led her into one of the bedrooms and started to kiss her. After awhile, he slipped off her T-shirt and she unzipped his jeans. She was feeling things she had never felt before. Ed was warm and gentle, and she felt so good to be with him. He got up from the bed and took a condom out of his jeans' pocket. That's when she began to feel confused. She really liked Ed and almost wanted to go all the way with him, but she was afraid, afraid of AIDS, afraid that if she did it this time, sex would become a part of every date they would have, afraid that Ed

What's Your Stress Level?

For most teenagers enduring life stresses are very much a part of life. How has your life been affected by them? Take a piece of paper and jot down answers to the following questions:

1. In the past three months what enduring life stresses have you faced?
2. What physical, emotional, behavioral, or mental stress symptoms did you exhibit?
3. What specific coping mechanisms did you employ?
4. Do your enduring life stresses seem to cluster in one particular category? (academic achievement stressors, social relationship stressors, family relationship stressors, future concern stressors)
5. What enduring life stresses do you anticipate experiencing in the near future?
6. How can you prepare for them in order to minimize their negative effect upon you?

would realize that this was her first time, but also afraid that if she stopped things now, Ed would start dating someone else. She was not prepared for this; she had not thought it through. She wished that she never got herself into this compromising situation, and she felt that she was just a stupid, ugly freshman and that if Ed stopped dating her she would be miserable. She just wanted to run away and pretend all this had never happened.

Angela closed her eyes and said, "Ed, I can't, not now . . . I'm just not ready . . . Please don't hate me."

She was afraid to open up her eyes, so she turned her head away from Ed and got up off the bed. She tried to concentrate on getting dressed. Her hands were shaking a little, and she was choking back the tears. She kept her head down and would not look at Ed. She stood by the bedroom door and waited for him to get dressed. They left the party, and Ed drove her home in total silence. She felt very awkward and when he pulled up to her house, she was crying and had a terrible headache. She had wanted to say something but didn't know what to say; so instead, she just got out of the car and ran up to her front door.

As she sat in her bedroom, Angela's head was throbbing, and she kept going over what had happened and wishing that it just never happened.

Angela is having a difficult time dealing with her sexuality. Her feeling of being overwhelmed and of being "stupid and ugly" are symptoms of the intense stress she is suffering. Angela is using emotional coping strategies to deal with the pain she is experiencing. She is desperately trying to deny that the whole incident took place, but her throbbing headache and the fact that she continues to replay the event in her mind are symptoms of the tremendous stress she is feeling.

Angela needs to look at her date with Ed more realistically to affirm and accept the fact that she is not yet ready for sexual intimacy and to understand that it is okay. Like other young women her age, she may be experiencing peer pressure from Ed to take her relationship one step further. Her hesitancy is one indication that she does not want to take that step just now. Deciding to be sexually intimate has both emotional and physical consequences and should be a personal decision based on strong self-convictions and not peer pressure.

Tonight, Angela should let go of her self-doubt and try to get some sleep. By tomorrow she will have achieved some emotional distance from the event and will be better able to evaluate her actions. Important decisions, especially those having to do with a relationship and values, should not be made in haste. Often when they are made in haste, teens forgo their own values and cave in to peer pressure. Perhaps discussing the date with a close friend will help Angela hear her own thoughts and realize that her feelings and her wishes are important in a relationship. Talking to a friend can also bring out the fact that Angela did the right thing.

Angela also needs to talk with Ed. Communication within a relationship is extremely important. Ed should know just how Angela feels about going all the way.

5

Chronic Daily Stress

Donna woke up late, and it seemed as if she played catch-up all day. She hurriedly dressed for school and stopped off in the kitchen on her way out. She was reaching into the refrigerator when her little sister distracted her and Donna dropped the quart of milk. To make things even worse, as she was getting onto the school bus she tripped on the stairs and found herself sprawled on the floor of the bus while her books, wallet, and keys were scattered everywhere. When she got to school, she realized she had forgotten that she was having a Spanish quiz. As her day progressed, Donna felt as if she was stumbling through a series of mishaps, mistakes, and blunders.

A day like this—when annoying and upsetting events keep recurring—is terrible for any teenager.

Chronic Daily Stress

Chronic Daily Stress	Ways to Eliminate the Stress
Being late for class, work, or an activity	Set a watch five minutes ahead and make sure to go directly to the destination; do not stop to talk with friends or try to complete another errand on the way.
Forgetting to do homework	Write down all homework assignments in a small notebook daily.
Missing an important meeting	Keep a small pocket-size date book and mark important dates and times.
Not getting enough sleep	Start homework in the afternoon if possible and don't leave things until the last minute.
Being interrupted while working	When working on something important, try to find a quiet secluded place to work away from others.
Having problems with homework	Have a reliable study partner in each class; call them for help.
Being bothered by a younger sibling	Make plans to spend time with sibling later in the day and ask parents or others to take care of him or her for now.

This is definitely a day filled with *chronic daily stress*. In comparison to major life transitions and enduring life stress, chronic daily stress is less catastrophic, more frequent, and almost totally within an individual's control. Because it is such a frequent and constant part of an adolescent's life, chronic daily stress can cause many of the same negative effects as the two more serious types of stress. Remember, no matter how small or seemingly insignificant the demands of chronic daily stress seem, they cause a disruption in the normal functioning of the body and produce a number of biological changes. When a teen's normal heart rate, respiration, blood pressure, stomach acid secretion, and dilation of blood vessels are constantly being disrupted, the body's ability to recover and return to its normal state is jeopardized. The body's energy is depleted and the ability to withstand stress is reduced.

Of the three types of stress experienced by teens, chronic daily stress can be managed and even decreased. Many of the events that cause the body to trigger the General Adaptive Syndrome can be controlled. By choosing to make some small changes in their daily habits and routine, teens can eliminate a large amount of chronic daily stress. The chart on the next page lists examples of chronic daily stress that teens face and things that can be done to eliminate this stress.

Another way to eliminate chronic daily stress is to develop a stress buster list. Make a list of all of the chronic daily stresses experienced in a day. Then determine which chronic daily stress can be avoided and how to avoid it. Next reexamine the list and look at the chronic daily stresses that cannot be avoided. Now think of appropriate coping mechanisms to use

Stress Buster List

My Chronic Daily Stress

1. Cannot find the clothes I want to wear to school.
2. Nothing good to eat for breakfast.
3. Sister hogs the bathroom, and I'm stuck waiting to take my shower and do my hair.
4. Mother likes to talk to me in the morning. I hate to talk. I just want to eat and get to school.
5. Waiting in line at the school cafeteria.
6. Going to algebra class.
7. Listening to my sister play her stupid CDs.
8. Doing nightly homework.

Solutions:

(How I can avoid particular chronic daily stresses)

1. Decide the night before what to wear to school and put it out.
2. Tell mom what I want for breakfast when she is going food shopping and ask her to buy it.
3. Get up ten minutes earlier than my sister and get in the bathroom first.
4.–6. Cannot do anything about this (see coping strategy below★).
7. Ask sister to please turn down the volume or go to an area in the house where I cannot hear the CD.
8. Cannot do anything about this (see coping strategy below★).

★Coping strategies I can use when I cannot avoid a chronic daily stress

4. Accept the situation and recognize there is not much I can do to change it.
5. While standing in line try to take several slow deep breaths in and out to relieve the pressure.
6. Accept the situation and recognize there is not much I can do to change it.
8. Take a five-minute break every thirty minutes. During this five minutes, go outside and run around the yard or do twenty-five jumping jacks or just close my eyes and listen to my favorite song.

in order to deal with the anticipated stress. The list on the left-hand page is an example of a teenager's stress buster list.

Every teenager can make some minor adjustments and actually eliminate a large portion of the chronic daily stress present in his or her life. It is worth the effort!

6

Measure Your Stress

———————

In order to get a handle on the level of stress teenagers are experiencing, this chapter will provide an opportunity to measure your stress. If young people are aware of the things in their lives that cause stress, they can begin to determine how to eliminate or cope with the stress. This will enable teens to enjoy a healthy adolescence, become more responsible for the type of life they choose to lead, and develop a stronger sense of self-confidence.

Teens can experience several positive changes once they learn how to identify and deal with their stress. See the next page for examples of benefits gained by other teens who worked on getting their stress under control.

Measuring Your Stress

The following self-assessment is easy to do. It will help you identify areas within your life that are currently causing you stress. Take out a piece of paper. On the left side, number down the side from 1 to 20. Across the top of the page write 1 Point, leave a small space and write 2 Points, leave a small space again and write 3 Points. Read each statement and choose the response that most accurately applies to you. Indicate your answer on your paper. (Please do not write in or mark this book.)

My Stress Assessment

Friends	1 Point	2 Points	3 Points
1. I get along with the kids at school.	almost always	sometimes	hardly at all
2. I feel pressure from my friends to do things that I do not want to do.	hardly ever	sometimes	a lot
3. I argue with my boy/girlfriend.	infrequently	sometimes	frequently
4. I feel left out of activities and events that my friends participate in.	hardly ever	sometimes	most of the time

School	1 Point	2 Points	3 Points
5. I like to go to school.	almost always	sometimes	hardly ever
6. I am doing as well in school as I'd like.	most of the time	sometimes	hardly at all
7. My parents expect me to do better than I am doing.	hardly ever	sometimes	most of the time
8. I have problems in school.	almost never	sometimes	a lot
9. I often fall behind in my school assignments.	almost never	sometimes	most of the time

Family	1 Point	2 Points	3 Points
10. I get along with my parents.	almost always	sometimes	not very often
11. I get along with my brothers/sisters.	most of the time	sometimes	almost never
12. I feel that I am not able to live up to my parents' expectations.	hardly ever	sometimes	most of the time
13. My parents criticize me.	infrequently	sometimes	frequently
14. My parents are pleased with the friends I have.	almost always	sometimes	not very often

Self	1 Point	2 Points	3 Points
15. I feel safe in my home.	always	sometimes	hardly ever
16. I feel safe in my neighborhood.	most of the time	sometimes	hardly ever
17. I feel safe when I am at school.	most of the time	sometimes	not very often
18. My family has enough money to live on.	almost always	sometimes	hardly ever
19. I feel good about myself.	most of the time	sometimes	not very often
20. I worry about my future.	once in a while	sometimes	almost always

Now add up your score and write it at the bottom of your paper. If you have experienced a major life transition within the last six months, add 21 points to your score. This number is your total score. See pages 76–77 for the results of your score.

The Results

☐ If your total score is between 20 and 30, you currently have a low level of stress in your life. You seem to enjoy being with your friends. You have similar interests and participate in common activities. At school, you seem to enjoy learning and more often than not you are working to your potential. Your parents' expectations are in most cases similar to yours. You can handle most of the ups and downs of school life without a lot of difficulty. Your relationship with your family tends to be strong. Although there are times when you are in conflict with them, you and your parents usually get along. Your interactions with your siblings are harmonious most of the time, your parents seem to accept the way you are progressing through adolescence, and you seem to be comfortable with their parenting style. On the whole, you have a positive image of yourself. Your needs seem to be met, and you feel as if you have adequate control over your life.

☐ If your total score is between 31 and 40, you have moderate stress within your life. While this stress is not overwhelming, you may want to consider ways in which you can decrease it. If your stress is concentrated in the Friends area, you may want to consider how you interact with them. Are your interests similar to those of your friends? Do you feel comfortable voicing your opinion in front of them? Do your friends take into consideration your likes and dislikes when planning activities? Are these the friends you really want to be with? If your stress is concentrated in the School area, are you putting in the quality time necessary to understand and learn? Are you in classes that are above or below your academic level? Are there resources at school that you are not using that may help you to do better? Can you put up with the current situation until you graduate? If your stress is concentrated in the Family and/or Self areas, this will be a lot more difficult to alter. Not all teenagers live in a stable home environment, and in reality there is not much you can do to change this. You will have to develop some appropriate, effective coping mechanisms and employ stress reduction activities that will enable your body and mind to handle the stress.

- If your total score is between 41 and 50, your level of stress is above the moderate level and you may begin experiencing physical, emotional, behavioral, and/or mental symptoms of stress overload. You need to meet with your school counselor or other professional who can help you eliminate or cope with your stress. Try to remember that you are not alone, millions of other American teenagers are experiencing stressful life events. Most school counselors report a dramatic increase in the number of students who are seeking them out for counseling and assistance with life stressors. Help is available if you seek it out.

- If you scored 51 points or more, your life is very stressful and you probably are experiencing many symptoms of stress overload. Your body and mind functions are being severely compromised by the negative effects of stress. You should seek professional intervention as soon as possible! Speak to your parents or school counselor about ways you can find help.

Now that you know your stress score, you can decide if you want to do something about it. Here are some suggestions. Look at the four categories

(Friends, School, Family, Self) again. You will notice that in every category there are things you have control over and things that are out of your control. You have the power to change only those things that you can control, such as your attitude, your behavior, or your feelings. you cannot change your parents' expectations, their income, or where you live. Looking at the assessment, try to determine which categories are generating the most stress. Are you experiencing stress in all four areas or does your stress seem to cluster in only one or two categories? What are these

Benefits of Controlling Stress

- ☐ increase in energy
- ☐ less headaches
- ☐ reduction in the number of cigarettes smoked
- ☐ less frequent colds and sore throats
- ☐ improvement in physical appearance such as a clearer complexion, and decrease in nail-biting
- ☐ less difficulty making decisions
- ☐ crying less
- ☐ sleeping more restfully at night
- ☐ better concentration
- ☐ enjoying life more

categories? If your stress is reflected throughout all four categories, this indicates that there are stressful things that influence the four most influential aspects of your daily life. Are you able to handle this?

Next, go over each 3-point response you made. Is it within an area that you can control, such as your attitude, behavior, or feelings? If it is, do you want to change or modify your actions in order to eliminate some of the stress? If your stress is generated from an area that you have no control over, such as your parents' expectations, income level, or where you live, can you use an appropriate coping mechanism to offset some of the stress?

Now that you have a better idea of the sources of your stress and the amount of stress you are dealing with on a daily basis, what actions do you need to take in order to manage your stress? And, most importantly, are you willing to make the changes necessary to alter the amount of stress you are subjected to?

7

Stress Prevention

Problems occur when teenagers perceive that the demands from major life stress, enduring life stress, and chronic daily stress exceed the physical and mental resources they have at hand. Although stress is a natural part of all adolescent development, when stress levels are high teens become at risk for stress overload and all the physical, mental, psychological, and behavioral symptoms that occur with it. This overload doesn't always have to happen. There are three specific things teens can do to prevent stress overload. Teens can enhance their self-esteem and significantly diminish their sense of being in danger. They can develop a healthy lifestyle and increase their body's resources necessary to deal with stress, and they can learn to practice daily relaxation techniques.

What Is Self-Esteem and How Can It Reduce Stress?

Self-esteem is defined as "the evaluation which individuals make about themselves."[1] Teens who have a good self-image are comfortable with their accomplishments. They are confident in their abilities. They trust their own judgment and take responsibility for their own actions. These teens are conscious of both their strengths and weaknesses, and they are able to tolerate their mistakes and failures. Because they believe in themselves, they feel they can handle many things that would cause stress for teens who have low self-esteem. In addition, they tend not to blame themselves for events like major life transitions that are out of their control. Liz, Andy, and Annie, whose stories follow, are examples of teens who have a positive self-image and are able to handle typical life events that could potentially be stressful.

Self-esteem is a powerful and useful weapon in the struggle against stress overload and it is something all teenagers can construct and foster within themselves. It is not a characteristic that an individual is born with or born without. It is something each individual can create. Therefore, everyone has the potential to build up his or her self-esteem.

Liz

Liz's family was going to be moving in a few weeks. Her dad had been transferred to another state. She was sad to be leaving her best friend, Judy, but she knew that she would find a way to keep up her friendship with her. They would write every week and call each other several times a month. They were already making plans for Judy to come visit over winter vacation. Whenever Liz thought about moving, she tried to keep in mind that there were a lot of good things that were going to happen like being able to decorate her room the way she wanted. She looked at the move as an adventure and an opportunity to see another area of the country and learn about new things. She knew that at first she would be a little lonesome, but because she liked being with people she knew that she would make new friends easily.

Andy

Andy was sitting in study hall thinking about what would be happening that afternoon. At 4:00 P.M. he was going to the motor vehicle office to take his road test. If he passed, he would get his driver's license. He thought for a minute, "Of course I'm going to pass. I studied the manual and spent over twenty hours in driver's education class. I can handle the car well and know all the traffic rules. Why am I wasting my time thinking about this? I better try to finish my homework in study hall so tonight I'll be free to take the car over to Ed's house after supper."

Annie

Annie had been experiencing difficulties in algebra all year. She worked hard to understand the material but just could not do the work. She tried to keep up with the assignments but occasionally fell behind. By the end of the year it was apparent that Annie was going to flunk the course. After her final exam in algebra, Annie and her friend Betsy walked home together. Annie told Betsy that she would be going to summer school to make up the course. She had tried her best in math but just could not understand the material well enough to pass. She wasn't looking forward to going to summer school but said she accepted the fact that she had to go. "I just don't do well in math courses, but I'm pretty sure I got a *C* or better in all my other courses. I worked hard, even in my algebra class. And I feel pretty good about my grades in all my other subjects."

Building Self-Esteem

There are several ways teens can improve their self-esteem. One way is for adolescents to learn to like themselves. That means not being overly critical of the way they look and the things they do. Teens often do not look at themselves realistically. They tend to concentrate on their shortcomings and pass over their accomplishments. They can experience negative thoughts such as thinking they are stupid, or ugly, or untalented, or fall into the habit of putting themselves down. ("I'll never make the cheerleading squad. I'm so uncoordinated I fall over myself just trying to walk.") Teens who want to develop a strong sense of self-esteem do not let themselves fall into this trap. When they begin to experience negative thoughts about themselves, they stop immediately and replace those thoughts with ones that are less judgmental and more realistic. Here is an example: No one is really stupid, but everyone has subjects they cannot understand. No one is capable of doing everything wrong, but everyone does make some mistakes. No one is useless, but there are things that some people just cannot do.

Another way teens can boost their self-esteem is by

developing a close relationship or friendship with someone with whom they can share their thoughts, actions, and feelings. A strong friendship provides the companionship and caring necessary for teens to believe in themselves. With the support of a friend a teen can accomplish and endure things more easily. In addition, when a teenager provides support for a friend, he or she experiences an increase in his or her own sense of self-worth and feelings of fulfillment. Having a good friend and being a good friend is a definite step toward strengthening self-esteem.

Yet another way teens can increase their self-esteem is by trying to make the best of each day. That means not wasting time feeling sorry for the things they messed up yesterday or worrying about the problems they may be facing tomorrow. Instead, teens who have self-esteem try to use their energy to anticipate and plan for each day's events. Instead of brooding on past mistakes, they view their mistakes as learning experiences. They take each day in stride, enjoying those things that can be fun and not dwelling on things that make them angry or sad.

How a Healthy Lifestyle Can Reduce Stress

Stress depletes the body of energy. The more energy one has, the more stress the person can handle. Body energy is at its maximum when individuals are healthy. Unfortunately, teenagers are notorious for poor health habits. They are also being bombarded by stressful situations on a daily basis. So teens face a real challenge in the battle against stress. Although most teenagers have some knowledge of how to live a healthier life, most choose to ignore this knowledge

Tips for Staying Healthy

Eat the right foods. During adolescence your body is using much of its energy to grow. You need protein to build muscle, calcium to build bones, carbohydrates to provide energy, and vitamins to provide essential elements. Eat foods like lean meat, fish or chicken, pasta and beans, lots of vegetables and whole grains, fresh fruits, and low-fat dairy products. Stay away from fried foods.

Get the amount of rest you need to function at your best level. Some teens need more than eight hours of sleep a night; very few need less than eight hours. For most of the year, teens are up and out of the house between 7:00 and 8:00 A.M. on weekdays. They have a full day of activities that require mental and physical alertness. They are literally on the go for twelve to fifteen hours a day. They must have adequate sleep each day to renew their body energy.

Participating in recreational exercise is an important aspect of being healthy. Today, teens are less likely to walk or ride a bike to school or events and more likely to spend time sitting in front of the TV or a computer. Teens need to engage in some type of physical activity they enjoy on a regular basis—one that will increase heart rate, improve blood circulation, and provide a workout for the entire body.

Healthy teens do not smoke, drink alcohol, or use drugs.

and develop unhealthy habits, especially during their preteen years. These habits include cigarette smoking, drinking, choosing to eat junk foods high in sugar and fat and low in necessary nutrients, eating and drinking foods with high quantities of caffeine, not getting enough sleep, failing to exercise, and even using illegal drugs. All teenagers have a choice. They can deny their bodies the energy they need to combat stress. Or they can shed poor health habits and develop more stress-resistant habits.

What Is Relaxation and How Can It Help Me?

Relaxation is defined as "a natural and innate protective mechanism against 'overstress,' which allows us to turn off harmful bodily effects. . . . This response against 'overstress' brings on bodily changes that decrease heart rate, lower metabolism, decrease the rate of breathing and bring the body back into what is probably a healthier balance."[2]

As early as 1934, Edmund Jacobson developed a series of relaxation exercises that were used to combat tension and anxiety.[3] In the late 1940s, Joseph Wolpe expanded the relaxation studies and actually developed a series of relaxation exercises that changed the way the body reacts when under stress.[4] In the 1960s, Husek and Alexander measured muscle tension, heart rate, skin conductance, and respiration rate on people in stressful situations (Remember that during the arousal state of the General Adaptive Syndrome heart rate increases, respiration deepens, and circulation to the skin decreases.) and found that people who employed relaxation exercises had a

Kick Back and Relax!

Set aside a special time each day (about twenty minutes) to practice relaxation exercises. Make sure it is around the same time every day, and do not let anything interfere with this time.

☐ Seek out a comfortable, quiet place to be alone while doing the exercises, and make sure you cannot hear the phone or any noises that may distract you. Try and use the same place every day.

☐ You may want to play music you enjoy and music that will soothe you while you are doing your relaxation exercise.

☐ Stay focused throughout the relaxation period and concentrate on breathing slowly and letting the tension flow out of your body.

☐ Do not worry about how or what you look like, or whether you are doing everything correctly.

☐ Remember that relaxation is a powerful way of managing stress.

significant reduction in heart rate, muscle tension, and respiration rate.[5] Relaxation exercises were able to inhibit or block these three physical changes that take place during the General Adaptive Syndrome.

In the 1970s Dr. Herbert Benson put together most of the scientific research that had been done about relaxation and published the information in a book called *The Relaxation Response*. Benson scientifically concluded that proper relaxation exercises offer a natural balance to counteract the undesirable manifestations of the General Adaptive Syndrome.[6]

Relaxation may be the easiest and most successful way in which teens can counteract the physical and mental effects of stress. Although relaxation can be achieved through many different ways, the most important aspect of any type of relaxation is that it creates a state of being in which the body actually experiences physiological and psychological changes activated by the nervous system. Being able to relax is a skill that takes some practice to attain. The more teens practice, the longer the feeling of being relaxed will stay with them. It may take several days of relaxation exercises in order to begin experiencing noticeable changes, but in the end it is worth the time and effort. Relaxation can and does help manage stress because it allows the body to move out of the General Adaptive Syndrome and return to a more normal state. That means that as a teen's arousal level is lowered he or she is less likely to react to additional stressors. Relaxation allows teenagers to react more calmly during stressful situations and turns other daily unavoidable problems into less stressful events. Relaxation definitely helps teenagers to make it through a stressful event and to choose more appropriate coping mechanisms.

When teenagers experience a state of relaxation after a stressful incident, they can lessen most of the physical, emotional, behavioral, and mental symptoms of stress. Relaxation can also help teenagers become more sensitive to their physical responses to stress and allow them to feel the difference between tension and relaxation.

Teens and Stress

Teens can control the stress within their lives. It will take effort, time, and practice, but the investment is worth it. Here are a few things to remember.

There are three types of stress that adolescents experience. Major life transitions are the most serious and the ones that teens have no control over. If a teen is experiencing a major life transition, he or she should seek help from a parent or a professional counselor. Enduring life stress revolves around a teen's interaction with his or her environment, family, friends, activities, and enemies. Teens can control or modify many of the factors that contribute to this type of stress. Chronic daily stress is the most common type of teen stress and the easiest to avoid. Teens can decrease the occurrence of chronic daily stress by changing some of their behaviors.

When teens experience stress, the best way to deal with it is to activate the four-step model for coping with stress. Through the model they will accurately evaluate the stress experience, review the possible combinations of cognitive, emotional, or practical strategies to use, activate the proper combinations of coping strategies, and ultimately return their bodies to a normal rate of functioning.

There are three specific ways in which teens can protect themselves from stress overload. They can consciously develop a strong sense of self-esteem. They can choose to live a healthier lifestyle and they can incorporate a session of relaxation exercises (see pages 91–93) into their day.

Relaxation Exercises

This series of deep muscle relaxation exercises should take about twenty minutes to complete. No special equipment is needed and most parts of this series can be done independently when you feel you need a shorter stress break. But for best results try to fit a twenty-minute relaxation session into your daily schedule. In this way you will receive the maximum benefit from relaxation.

To begin your relaxation exercises all you need is a comfortable straight-backed chair and a quiet place. Each set of exercises concentrates on one area of the body. If you are doing the entire series, try and keep your eyes closed and your mind free of any thoughts or worries. Start with the Hands and Arms exercise. If you want to use a set or two for shorter stress breaks during the day, the Hands and Arms, Jaw, Stomach, and Legs and Feet series can easily be done almost anywhere.

At the end of the deep muscle relaxation series, stay as relaxed as you can. Try and let your whole body go limp and feel all your muscles relax. Enjoy the sensation for a minute or two!

Hands and Arms

Make a fist with your left hand. Squeeze it hard and count slowly to four. Feel the tightness in your hand and arm as you squeeze. Now, let your fingers and hand relax, and slowly count to six. See how much better your hand and arm feel when they are relaxed. Repeat this exercise on your left hand five times, then on your right hand and arm five times, and then do both sides together five times.

Hand and arm exercises can be done sitting or standing. They are an ideal exercise to do to break the tension while you are waiting in line.

Arms and Shoulders

Stand up straight and stretch your arms out in front of you. Raise your arms high up over your head and back. Feel how your shoulders pull. Keep stretching and slowly count to four. Now let your arms drop down to your side. Count to six, then shake both arms for a second. Slowly raise them over your head again and pull them back. Count to four slowly. Can you feel them pulling? Now let them drop. Feel how good it is to let them relax. Count to six slowly and shake both arms. Repeat this exercise eight times.

Shoulders and Neck

While sitting in a chair or standing, try to pull your shoulders up to your ears and push your head down into your shoulders. Hold it tight and slowly count to four. Now relax and let your shoulders fall into place. Feel the tensions flowing away. Count to six and again pull your shoulders up to your ears and push your head down into your shoulders. Hold it to a count of four and relax. Feel how comfortable it is to relax. Try to repeat this exercise eight times.

Stomach

This exercise can be done standing, sitting, or lying down. Tighten your stomach muscles really tightly and try to make them as tight as you can. Hold it for a slow count of four. Now relax and let your stomach go soft and count slowly to six. This time as you tighten your stomach try and tighten it so much that it feels as if it were pushing up against your backbone. Pull it in and hold it for a count of four. Now relax and feel your muscles going soft and loose. Count slowly to six and repeat this exercise. Try to complete this exercise eight times. The stomach relaxation exercise is another stress relaxation exercise that can be done almost anywhere.

Face and Neck

Wrinkle up your nose. Try to squeeze your lips, cheek, nose, and forehead together and tightly close your eyes. Hold it tight and slowly count to four. Now release. This time when you begin to wrinkle your nose notice how it also makes your lips, eyelids, cheeks, and forehead pucker up. Squeeze hard, slowly count to four and relax. Count to six and repeat. Try to do this exercise eight times. When you are done, notice how smooth and relaxed your whole face feels.

Jaw

Put your teeth together really hard. Let your neck muscles help you to tighten your jaw. Count to four and release. Let your jaw hang loosely and slowly count to six. See how good it feels just to let go and relax. Now, put your teeth together again, bite down as hard as you can, count to four and release. Do this exercise eight times. Jaw exercises can be done almost anywhere, while waiting in line, while taking a test, or while listening to a lecture or studying in the library.

Legs and Feet

While sitting in a straight-back chair, push your toes on your left foot down really hard on to the floor. Use your leg muscles to push as hard as you can, and while you are pushing spread your toes apart. Push hard and count to four. Now relax your left foot and count to six. As you relax, wiggle your toes. Doesn't it feel good to relax? Now try it with your right foot. Push those toes on your right foot as hard as you can onto the floor and try to spread them out while pushing. Push hard and count to four. Now relax. Try to do this exercise eight times on each foot and four times on both feet together.

Where to Find Help

Sources of Help for Teens
Dealing With Stress

It is estimated that 7 million youth (one in four adolescents) are at increased risk for stress overload and that these teenagers show a significant increase in psychological, physical, emotional, and behavioral problems at home and in school. If teenagers find themselves overwhelmed by the stress in their lives, they should look beyond themselves and their circle of friends for help. Professional help is available in many areas.

Most students have access to a school guidance counselor. In addition to being trained in academic scheduling, educational theory, and college/career development, guidance counselors are one of the primary support staff for adolescents. School counselors engage students in problem-solving and decision-making skills that center around personal, social, and educational issues. They are concerned with the mental health of each student and through confidentiality, student advocacy, counseling, building self-esteem, and educating students, school counselors can be a real source of help for students dealing with stress and a resource of information on area agencies and organizations that provide help for teenagers.

Your local public library is also a wonderful source of information. Books, journals, videos, and pamphlets about all the issues and problems teens face are available along with information about local agencies and organizations that can provide help.

In addition, a number of national organizations offer pamphlets, referrals, groups, and resources that can be of use to teenagers. Listed below are the names and addresses of some national organizations teens can contact for help in specific areas that may be causing stress within their lives.

1. **ALCOHOLICS ANONYMOUS**
   Box 495 Grand Central Station
   New York, NY 10163
   212-870-3400

2. **AL-ANON FAMILY GROUPS/ALATEEN (for families of alcoholics)**
   1600 Corporate Landing Parkway
   Virginia Beach, VA 23454-5617
   800-356-9996

3. **NARCOTICS ANONYMOUS**
   1935 South Myrtle Avenue
   Monrovia, CA 91016-4855
   (818)-359-0084; 800-896-8896

4. **OURS (a free self-help network that provides support and information for people in adoptive families) from Adoptive Families of America, Inc.**
   3307 Highway 100 North
   Minneapolis, MN 55422
   612-535-4829; 800-372-3300

5. **NATIONAL INFORMATION CENTER FOR CHILDREN AND YOUTH WITH DISABILITIES**
   P.O. Box 1492
   Washington, DC 20013-1492
   202-884-8200; 800-695-0285

6. **THE COLLEGE BOARD** (provides free information on college admission and financial aid)
45 Columbus Ave.
New York, NY 10023
212-713-8000

7. **COMPASSIONATE FRIENDS** (association for parents and siblings of a child who has died)
P.O. Box 3696
Oak Brook, IL 60522-3696
708-990-0010

8. **STEPFAMILY ASSOCIATION OF AMERICA**
215 Centennial Mall South
Suite 212
Lincoln, NB 68508
402-477-7837; 800-735-0329

The following books and audiotapes can be borrowed from the school or public library.

1. Blumenfeld, Larry, ed. *The Big Book of Relaxation*. New York: The Relaxation Company, 1994.

2. McKay, Matthew. *Progressive Relaxation* (audiotape). California: New Haringer Publications, 1982.

3. Dyer, Wayne. *Relax and Enjoy Your Life* (audiotape). Illinois: Nightingale-Conan Corp., 1990.

4. Olesen, Erik. *Twelve Steps to Mastering the Winds of Change* (audiotape recording). Toronto: Rawson Associates, 1993.

5. *Ten Minutes to Relax*, vols. 1, 2, 3, 4 (audiotape). New York: The Relaxation Company, 1993.

Chapter Notes

Chapter 1

1. Tom Cox, *Stress* (Baltimore: University Press, 1981), p. 4.
2. Leo Goldberger and Shlomo Breznitz, *Handbook of Stress: Theoretical and Clinical Aspects* (New York: The Free Press, 1986), p. 369.
3. I. Lutash, *Handbook on Stress and Anxiety* (San Francisco: Jossey-Bass Publishers, 1980), p. 127.
4. Cox, p. 57.
5. Vernon Hamilton and David Warburton, *Human Stress and Cognition* (New York: John Wiley and Sons, 1981), p. 17.
6. Lutash, p. 133.
7. Cox, p. 94.
8. Goldberger and Breznitz, p. 165.
9. Ibid., p. 742.
10. Ibid., pp. 368–369.
11. Robert Berkow, *The Merck Manual* (New Jersey: Merck, Sharp & Dohme Research Laboratories, 1982), pp. 1906–1907.

Chapter 2

1. Donna Mates and Kenneth Allison, "Sources of Stress and Coping Responses of High School Students," *Adolescence*, vol. 27, no. 106, Summer 1992, pp. 463–474.
2. I. Lutash, *Handbook on Stress and Anxiety* (San Francisco: Jossey-Bass Publishers, 1980), pp. 212–230.
3. Michael Hoffman, Rachel Levy-Shiff, Shaul Sohlberg, and Julia Zariski, "The Impact of Stress and Coping," *Journal of Youth and Adolescence*, vol. 21, no. 4, 1991, pp. 531–544.

4. Leo Goldberger and Shlomo Breznitz, *Handbook of Stress: Theoretical and Clinical Aspects* (New York: The Free Press, 1986), p. 369.

Chapter 7

1. M. Rosenberg, *Society & the Adolescent Self-Image* (Hanover, N.H.: University Press of New England, 1989), p. 5.

2. Herbert Benson, *The Relaxation Response* (New York: William Morrow and Company, 1975), p. 18.

3. Douglas Bernstein and Thomas Borkovec, *Progressive Relaxation Training* (Illinois: Research Press, 1973), p. 3.

4. Ibid., p. 4.

5. Ibid., p. 5.

6. Benson, p. 121.

Further Reading

Books

Benson, Herbert. *The Relaxation Response.* New York: William Morrow and Company, 1975.

Berkow, Robert. *The Merck Manual.* New Jersey: Merck, Sharp & Dohme Research Laboratories, 1982.

Cohen, David, and Susan Cohen. *Teenage Stress.* New York, N.Y.: Bantam Doubleday Dell Books for Young Readers, 1992.

Colten, Mary E., and Susan Gore. *Adolescent Stress: Causes & Consequences.* Hawthorne, N.Y.: Aldine de Gruyter, 1991.

Cox, Tom. *Stress.* Baltimore: University Park Press, 1978.

Csikszentmihalyi, Mihaly, and Reed Larson. *Being Adolescent: Conflict & Growth in the Teenage Years.* New York, N.Y.: Basic Books, 1986.

Eliot, Robert. *From Stress to Strength.* New York: Bantam Books, 1993.

Forman, Susan. *Coping Skills Interventions for Children and Adolescents.* San Francisco: Jossey-Bass, 1990.

Gilbert, Sara. *Get Help: Solving the Problems in Your Life.* New York: Morrow Junior Books, 1989.

Goldberger, Leo, and Shlomo Breznitz. *Handbook of Stress: Theoretical and Clinical Aspects*. New York: The Free Press, 1982.

Hamilton, Vernon, and David Warburton, eds. *Human Stress and Cognition: An Information Processing Approach*. New York: John Wiley and Sons, 1981.

Lutash, I. *Handbook on Stress and Anxety*. San Francisco: Jossey-Bass Publishers, 1980.

Newman, Susan. *Don't Be S.A.D.: A Teenage Guide to Handling Stress, Anxiety & Depression*. Parsippany, N.J.: Simon and Schuster Trade, 1991.

Nourse, Alan E. *Teen Guide to Survival*. Danbury, Conn.: Franklin Watts Incorporated, 1990.

Ollendick, T. H., and J. Cerny. *Clinical Behavior Therapy with Children*. New York: Plenum Press, 1981.

Patel, Chandra. *The Complete Guide to Stress Management*. New York: Plenum Press, 1991.

Powell, Robin J. *The Working Woman's Guide to Managing Stress*. New Jersey: Prentice Hall, 1994.

Rosenberg, Morris, ed. *Society and the Adolescent Self-Image*. New Jersey: University Press of New England, 1989.

Ryan, Elizabeth A. *Straight Talk about Parents*. New York, N.Y.: Facts on File, Inc., 1989.

Pamphlets

An Introduction to Stress, No. 2005, Life Skills Education Series, 1995.

Coping With Family Stress, Life Skills Education Series, 1992.

Fit for Life, Life Skills Education Series, 1993.

Growing Self Esteem, Life Skills Education Series, 1994.

Living With Your Teenager, No. 2115, Life Skills Education Series, 1995.

Positively Making Optimism Work for You, Life Skills Education Series, 1992.

You and Your Self Image, No. 2001, Life Skills Education Series, 1995.

Articles

DuBois, David, Robert Felner, Stephen Brand, Angela Adam, and Elizabeth Evans. "A Prospective Study of Stress, Social Support, and Adaptation in Early Adolescence." *Child Development*, vol. 63, 542–557.

Hoffman, Michael, Rachel Levy-Shiff, Shaul Sohlberg, and Julia Zarizki. "The Impact of Stress and Coping." *Journal of Youth and Adolescence*, vol. 21, no. 4, 1992, 451–469.

Mates, Donna, and Kenneth Allison. "Sources of Stress and Coping Responses of High School Students." *Adolescence*, vol. 27, no. 106, (Summer 1992), 463–474.

Spirito, Anthony, Lori Stark, Nancy Grace, and Dean Stamoulis. "Common Problems and Coping Strategies Reported in Childhood and Early Adolescence." *Journal of Youth and Adolescence*, vol. 20, no. 5, 1991, 531–544.

Index